Earth Day

by Marc Tyler Nobleman

Content Adviser: Laura O'Laughlin, Coordinator,
USA Programs and Environmental Education,
Earth Day Network, Washington, D.C.

Reading Adviser: Susan Kesselring, M.A., Literacy Educator,
Rosemount-Apple Valley-Eagan (Minnesota) School District

Let's See Library
Compass Point Books
Minneapolis, Minnesota

Compass Point Books
3109 West 50th Street, #115
Minneapolis, MN 55410

Visit Compass Point Books on the Internet at *www.compasspointbooks.com*
or e-mail your request to *custserv@compasspointbooks.com*

On the cover: Half Dome in Yosemite National Park in California

Photographs ©: W. Cody/Corbis, cover; Fotopic/Index Stock Imagery, 4; Unicorn Stock Photos/Rich Baker, 6; Alex
Wong/Getty Images, 8; AP/Wide World Photos, 10; Digital Vision, 12, 20; USDA/ARS/Scott Bauer, 14; Skjold
Photographs, 16; Warren Morgan/Corbis, 18.

Creative Director: Terri Foley
Managing Editor: Catherine Neitge
Editors: Brenda Haugen and Christianne Jones
Photo Researcher: Marcie C. Spence
Designers: Melissa Kes and Les Tranby
Educational Consultant: Diane Smolinski

Library of Congress Cataloging-in-Publication Data
Nobleman, Marc Tyler.
    Earth Day / by Marc Tyler Nobleman.
        v. cm. — (Let's see)
    Includes bibliographical references and index.
    Contents: What is Earth Day?—When is Earth Day?—Who created Earth Day?—When did Earth Day begin?—What
did Earth Day change?—What issues are important on Earth Day?—What events occur on Earth Day?—How can I help on
Earth Day?—What does Earth Day mean to people?
    ISBN 0-7565-0645-X (Hardcover)
    1. Earth Day–Juvenile literature. 2. Environmental protection–Juvenile literature. [1. Earth Day. 2.Environmental
protection. 3. Holidays.] I. Title. II.Series.
    GE195.5.N63 2004
    333.72—dc22   2003023607

Table of Contents

NOTE: In this book, words that are defined in the glossary
*are in **bold** the first time they appear in the text.*

What Is Earth Day?

People celebrate our planet on Earth Day. They work together to help the **environment**. They clean up their communities.

Earth Day began in the United States. Today, people all around the world have this holiday.

Earth Day is not a day off for schools, post offices, banks, government offices, and companies. Yet no matter where people are on this special day, they know it's everyone's job to take care of our planet.

◄ Two boys put papers in a recycling bin.

When Is Earth Day?

Earth Day is every April 22. If April 22 is a weekday, people sometimes have special events during the weekend before or the weekend after Earth Day.

In some places, people make Earth Day longer. They celebrate Earth Week or even Earth Month.

Some people have another Earth Day on the first day of spring in the **Northern Hemisphere**. The first day of spring changes from year to year, but it is around March 21.

Many people believe the message of Earth Day is too important for only one day. They believe everyone should help the earth all the time. They say, "Earth Day is every day."

◄ *Members of a recycling committee give out free tree seedlings.*

Who Created Earth Day?

Gaylord Nelson started Earth Day.

Nelson was born in 1916. He has had many important jobs. He worked in the Wisconsin Senate. He was elected governor of Wisconsin. He was a United States senator for 18 years.

Nelson was worried about the environment. Factories, cars, and cities had caused **pollution**. He knew this was bad for humans, animals, and plants.

Nelson came up with the idea for Earth Day in the early 1960s. He tried to get people to support his idea. It took many years before they did.

◀ *Former Wisconsin Senator Gaylord Nelson*

When Did Earth Day Begin?

The first Earth Day was April 22, 1970. Denis Hayes was in charge of Earth Day for the whole country. He helped Gaylord Nelson plan the events. Nelson and Hayes started a new holiday.

People thought Earth Day was a great idea. Twenty million people around the United States went to Earth Day activities. Many of those people were students from thousands of schools.

People gathered peacefully in parks. They listened to speeches. They cleaned up litter. They showed the country's leaders that they wanted a healthier environment.

◄ *Denis Hayes in the Washington, D.C., office where he helped plan 1970's Earth Day*

What Did Earth Day Change?

Earth Day made people think about the environment. They wanted to make a difference. Earth Day caused the United States government to pass many laws to protect the environment.

The Environmental Protection Agency (EPA) was formed in 1970. Soon, laws were passed to protect the air and water from becoming polluted.

The Endangered Species Act was passed in 1973. This law protects plants and animals. It also protects animals' habitats, the places where they live. The Endangered Species Act helps make sure plants and animals will not become **extinct**.

◄ *Sea otters are among the animals protected by the Endangered Species Act.*

What Issues Are Important on Earth Day?

Earth Day was created to save the planet from more harm. So all environmental issues are important on Earth Day.

Scientists try to find better and safer methods to grow food and make energy. They try to find ways to prevent **waste**. They look for ways to get rid of pollution in the air, water, and soil.

Scientists work on ways to get rid of insect pests without using harmful **pesticides**.

People also try to stop deforestation, which is chopping down lots of trees in one place.

◄ *Scientists look at an insect trap made from papaya fruit.*

What Events Occur on Earth Day?

On Earth Day, people speak out against all types of pollution. They listen to ideas about how to fix the environment. They go to rallies. A rally is a big gathering of people who are working toward the same goal. Sometimes they wear clothes that have Earth Day sayings on them.

Communities host Earth Day parades, concerts, and festivals. People plant trees. Schools run Earth Day programs. These are fun events with a serious message. They ask people to keep the earth clean, now and into the future.

◄ *People work together to plant a tree.*

How Can I Help on Earth Day?

There are many ways to help the environment. You do not even have to leave home.

You can recycle. Many things can be recycled, including cans, plastic bottles, and newspapers. Communities often have recycling pick-up services.

Use cloth napkins instead of paper napkins. This cuts down on paper waste. Turn off the lights when you leave a room. This cuts down on energy waste. Do not leave the water running when you brush your teeth. This cuts down on water waste. Walk or ride a bicycle with your family instead of going in a car. This cuts down on air pollution.

◄ *A family bicycles instead of riding in a car.*

What Does Earth Day Mean to People?

Earth Day is a holiday of hope. It is a symbol of the future. On Earth Day, people stop and think about the planet. They enjoy the earth's beauty and work to keep it clean. They see that every person can make a difference. Even small actions can have big effects.

Our planet gives us life. Sometimes we forget this. Earth Day is only one day, but it reminds people that taking care of our planet every day is important.

◀ *Maroon Lake in the Rocky Mountains in Colorado*

Glossary

environment—natural surroundings such as air, water, and wildlife

extinct—no longer existing

Northern Hemisphere—the half of Earth that is above, or north of, the equator; the United States is one of the countries in the Northern Hemisphere

pesticides—chemicals used to keep animals and insects from eating plants

pollution—waste that people put into the water, land, and air

waste—garbage

Did You Know?

✶ On the first Earth Day, John Lindsay, the mayor of New York City, closed busy Fifth Avenue to automobiles for two hours. He wanted to show how clean and quiet a street without cars could be.

✶ World Environment Day is another special time to remember how important the earth is. In 1972, the United Nations chose June 5 of every year to be World Environment Day. On this day, world leaders make promises to take care of the earth now and into the future. People also plant trees, plan clean-up days, and hold bicycle parades.

✶ Clean Up the World weekends are held in September in many parts of the world. The event started in Australia after Ian Kiernan organized a clean-up of Sydney Harbor. Now people in many countries celebrate Clean Up the World weekends by picking up trash near where they live.

✶ In 1990, people in 141 countries took part in the 20th anniversary of Earth Day. By 2000, people in 184 countries celebrated Earth Day.

Want to Know More?

In the Library

Douglas, Lloyd G. *Let's Get Ready for Earth Day.* New York: Children's Press, 2003.

Gray, Shirley W. *Wetlands.* Minneapolis: Compass Point Books, 2001.

Margaret, Amy. *Earth Day.* New York: Power Kids Press, 2002.

Rau, Dana Meachen. *Earth.* Minneapolis: Compass Point Books, 2003.

On the Web

For more information on *Earth Day,* use FactHound to track down Web sites related to this book.

1. Go to *www.facthound.com*
2. Type in a search word related to this book or this book ID: 075650645X.
3. Click on the *Fetch It* button.

Your trusty FactHound will fetch the best Web sites for you!

On the Road

Colburn Earth Science Museum
2 South Pack Square
Asheville, NC 28801
828/254-7162
To learn about the earth and its resources

Many children's and science museums have annual Earth Day exhibits and events. Check the ones closest to you. If they don't have Earth Day events, suggest one!

Index

About the Author

Marc Tyler Nobleman has written more than 40 books for young readers. He has also written for a History Channel show called "The Great American History Quiz" and for several children's magazines including *Nickelodeon, Highlights for Children,* and *Read* (a Weekly Reader publication). He is also a cartoonist, and his single panels have appeared in more than 100 magazines internationally. He lives in Connecticut.